Happy Anniversary

ELLYN SANNA

*To love is to
receive a glimpse of heaven.*

KAREN SUNDE

An anniversary prayer for two special people:

As you continue your life journey together,
may you receive God's blessings of
love
beauty
harmony
wisdom.

Happy Anniversary

*See to it that
you really do love each other warmly,
with all your hearts.*

1 PETER 1:22 TLB

1

Love

Love never fails.

1 CORINTHIANS 13:8

A wedding is just an event,
the specific date on which promises were made
and words of commitment spoken.
A marriage is a lifetime journey
where promises are kept
and commitments fulfilled.

Happy Anniversary

Your anniversary is a celebration
of another milestone on that journey.
Look back and see how far you've come.
Look ahead and anticipate the joys that still lie ahead.
Rejoice in the love that has carried you so far,
and have confidence that it will endure
for the path that leads into the future.

Love alone is what gives value to all things.

TERESA OF AVILA

*It is always a feast where love is,
and where love is, God is.*

DOROTHY DAY

*Dear friends, let us practice loving each other,
for love comes from God and those who are loving and kind
show they are the children of God.*

1 JOHN 4:7 TLB

We love because he first loved us.

1 JOHN 4:19

*D*are to love and to be a real friend.
The love you give and receive is a reality
that will lead you closer and closer to God
as well as to those whom God has given you to love.

HENRI NOUWEN

How can we know God's love?
We know God's love through the human love we see.
Your love for each other shows God to the world.

Happy Anniversary

I love you the more
in that I believe you have liked me for my own sake
and for nothing else.

JOHN KEATS

*What's the earth with all its art, verse, music, worth
Compared with love, found, gained, and kept?*

ROBERT BROWNING

*E*very house where love abides
and friendship is a guest is surely a home,
and home sweet home; for there the heart can rest.

HENRY VAN DYKE

Love finds joy in living.
Love finds joy in giving.
Love finds joy in sharing.

I pray the two of you will continue
to find the joy of love in your life.
May your anniversary day be blessed with love.

*L*ove is extravagant in the price it is willing to pay,
the time it is willing to give,
the hardships it is willing to endure,
and the strength it is willing to spend.
Love never thinks in terms of "how little,"
but always in terms of "how much."
Love gives, love knows, love lasts.

Joni Eareckson Tada

So, chosen by God for this new life of love,
dress in the wardrobe God picked out for you:
compassion, kindness, humility, quiet strength, discipline.

Colossians 3:12 *The Message*

True love is eternal.
A friendship in which heart speaks to heart is a gift from God,
and no gift that comes from God is temporary or occasional.
All that comes from God participates in God's eternal life.

Henri Nouwen

May you find yourselves falling in love
over and over
and over again.

*It is a gift of God to us
to be able to share our love. . . .*

MOTHER TERESA

2

Beauty

Your beauty. . .should be that of your inner self,
the unfading beauty of a gentle and quiet spirit.

1 PETER 3:3–4

A marriage is made of such everyday things:
ordinary days begun with a smile,
a loving word, a shared meal.
Each day holds work to do,
appointments to keep, people to see.
All such ordinary things,
and yet all are wrapped in beauty
when they are carried out with love and commitment.

Happy Anniversary

Some days there is more commitment than love.
Other times commitment and love run neck and neck.
There may even be days when you ask,
"Where has love gone?"
Commitment stands firm even then.
Each day ends with a smile, a loving word,
a soft place to lay your heads. . .
and your hearts.
Such ordinary things
can be so beautiful.

Anything, everything, little or big
becomes an adventure
when the right person shares it.

KATHLEEN NORRIS

*May your life together be
a beautiful adventure!*

Love makes everything lovely.

GEORGE MACDONALD

There's beauty all around our paths, if our watchful eyes
Can trace it 'midst familiar things. . . .

MRS. HEMANS

A thing of beauty is a joy forever:
Its loveliness increases; it will never
Pass into nothingness. . . .

JOHN KEATS

21

The beauty you find in your life together
is a glimpse of grace.
It is God's hand touching your lives.
Make more room in your lives for that grace. . .
and you will find your love growing ever more beautiful.
Your marriage will become a room in the kingdom of God,
enriching all those who enter.

*G*od passes through the thicket of the world,
and wherever His glance falls He turns all things to beauty.

JOHN OF THE CROSS

How goodness heightens beauty!

HANNAH MORE

*T*he Kingdom of God is beauty.

NICOLAS BERDYAEV

*There is a daily round for beauty
as well as for goodness.*

CAROLINE C. GRAVESON

Wherever ugliness is kept at bay,
there the Spirit of God,
who is the God of Beauty,
is doing his creative and re-creative labour.

DONALD COGGAN

Happy Anniversary

In the year ahead,
make room for beauty in your life together.
You do not have to wait for it,
as though it were an accident, a coincidence,
over which you had no control.
Instead, when you choose to open your hearts to one another,
beauty will grow in your marriage. . .
and God will be present in your lives.

When beauty fires the blood,
how love exalts the mind.

JOHN DRYDEN

Now let us do something beautiful for God.

MOTHER TERESA

3

Harmony

*I*f two of you on earth agree about anything you ask for, it will be done for you by my Father in heaven.

MATTHEW 18:19

*Remember that happiness is a way of travel—
not a destination.*

ROY M. GOODMAN

Sometimes the married life is full of chasms
and rivers to cross
that make the journey difficult.
Keep your eyes on the path,
and seek the stepping-stones that lead to harmony.
These small stones are firm and steady,
though easily missed sometimes in the rush of life.

A smile,
a hug,
a kind gesture,
a helping hand,
a word of affirmation,
a place to feel secure and safe,
a heart that always gives.
These are the stepping-stones to harmony.

As you celebrate your life together,
may each past year become for you
another stepping-stone of strength and love
to lead you through the years ahead.

*We all stumble, every one of us.
That's why it's a comfort to go hand in hand.*

EMILY KIMBROUGH

Happy Anniversary

*A gentle answer turns away wrath,
but a harsh word stirs up anger.*

PROVERBS 15:1

Having someone who understands you is home.
Having someone who loves you is belonging.
Having both is a blessing.

ANONYMOUS

*Share each other's troubles and problems,
and so obey our Lord's command.*

GALATIANS 6:2 TLB

30

The point of love is to make us grow,
not to make us immediately happy.

MARIANNE WILLIAMSON

*In marriage each situation, each change,
offers a challenge and a triumph wrapped as one.
Marriage makes us grow into something better,
something finer,
something more.*

I used to believe that marriage would diminish me,
reduce my options.
That you had to be someone less to live with someone else
when, of course, you have to be someone more.

CANDICE BERGEN

Harmony's secret ingredients:

honest communication,
faithful commitment,
willingness to compromise,
and a celebration of differences.
These secrets build a marriage that does more than survive.
Together they create a marriage that thrives.

Communication means sharing together
of what you really are.
With the stethoscope of love
you listen until you hear
the heartbeat of the other.

ANONYMOUS

4

Wisdom

*Wisdom. . .is more profitable than silver
and yields better returns than gold.*

PROVERBS 3:13–14

The journey of marriage reveals
new discoveries at every turn.
Over and over, year after year,
you find out something new about each other.
But you will only find these treasures by looking
with fresh eyes and an open heart.
The wisest marriages celebrate each new year
as a time for discovery;
a chance to unwrap the mystery of the other person
just a little more.

*By wisdom a house is built,
and through understanding it is established.*

PROVERBS 24:3

*W*ho is wise and understanding? . . .
Let him show it by his good life,
by deeds done in the humility that comes from wisdom.
The wisdom that comes from heaven is first of all pure;
then peace-loving, considerate, submissive,
full of mercy and good fruit, impartial and sincere.

JAMES 3:13, 17

What marriage really means. . .
helping one another to reach the full status of being persons,
responsible and autonomous beings who
do not run away from life.

PAUL TOURNIER

*Good company on a journey makes
the way seem the shorter.*

IZAAK WALTON

May you each build the other up in wisdom,
learning from one another as you travel through the years.

Intimacy may not be rushed. . . .
Inwardness is time-consuming,
open only to minds willing to sample. . .
in small bites, savoring each one.

CALVIN MILLER

For this reason. . .
we have not stopped praying for you
and asking God to fill you with the knowledge of his will
through all spiritual wisdom and understanding.

COLOSSIANS 1:9

*K*nowledge is proud that he has learned so much;
Wisdom is humble. . . .

WILLIAM COWPER

Wisdom requires a surrender. . . .

GERHARD VON RAD

*B*e both wise and simple.

JOHN CHRYSOSTOM

*W*isdom. . .is a tree of life to those who hope in her. . . .
This tree of life into which we have to be grafted is Christ
who is the power and wisdom of God—
Christ who by His death,
that unprecedented gift of divine love,
became for us a tree of life.

ORIGEN

As an anniversary gift,
I pray that God will grant
that your marriage be grounded in wisdom. . .
grounded in Christ.

Thank You, God, for the years these two have shared,
days of joy, kindness, gentleness, and peace. . .
and days of pain, sorrow, anger, and loneliness.
Even when times were hard,
each day You offered them a new beginning.
As they begin a new year together,
may they celebrate the achievement of their past,
as they anticipate the triumph of their future.
Give them love, beauty, harmony, and wisdom,
in all the years to come.
Amen.

*May the Lord continually bless you
with heaven's blessings
as well as with human joys.*

PSALM 128:5 TLB